At a Glance™ Series

DVD and Lesson Book

DVD Scales & Modes for the Bass

Written by Chad Johnson and Joe Charupakorn

Video Performers: Elton Bradman & Steven Hoffman

ISBN: 978-1-4584-9116-9

HAL•LEONARD®
CORPORATION

7777 W. BLUEMOUND RD. P.O. BOX 13819 MILWAUKEE, WI 53213

Visit Hal Leonard Online at
www.halleonard.com

TABLE OF CONTENTS

Introduction

Welcome to *DVD Scales & Modes for Bass*, from Hal Leonard's exciting At a Glance series. Not as in-depth and slow-paced as traditional method books, the material in *DVD Scales & Modes for Bass* is presented in a snappy and fun manner intended to have you grooving in virtually no time at all. Plus, the At a Glance series uses real songs by real artists to illustrate how the concepts you're learning are applied in some of the biggest hits of all time. For example, in *DVD Scales & Modes for Bass*, you'll learn bass lines from such classics as "Day Tripper" (The Beatles), "Sultans of Swing" (Dire Straits), "Get Up (I Feel Like Being) a Sex Machine" (James Brown), and more.

Additionally, each book in the At a Glance series comes with a DVD containing video lessons that correspond to the printed material. The DVD that accompanies this book contains four video lessons, each approximately 8 to 12 minutes in length, which correspond to each chapter. In these videos, ace instructors Elton Bradman and Steven Hoffman will show you in great detail everything from the notes on the neck to the scale shapes with which you can seriously lay down the groove. As you work through this book, try to play the examples first on your own; then check out the DVD for additional help or to see if you played them correctly. As the saying goes, "A picture is worth a thousand words." So be sure to use this invaluable tool on your quest in learning scales and modes up and down the bass neck.

MAJOR AND MINOR SCALE SHAPES

Almost every classic bass line you hear is built from the notes of a scale, so it makes sense that, in order to create your own bass lines, you need to be familiar with scales and how to play them on the bass. In this lesson, we'll take a look at two of the most common scales in music—the major and minor scales—and learn how to play them on bass. We'll also learn some great bass lines in the process.

What Is a Scale?

So, what is a scale? Well, it's basically a collection of notes that we use to form melodies, chords, or, in our case, bass lines. It's kind of like an alphabet. Just as we use 26 letters to create words, we use the seven notes of a scale to create our bass lines.

The Major Scale

Let's start with the major scale, which is undoubtedly the most common scale in all of Western music. We'll learn two different major scale shapes, each of which can be moved anywhere on the neck to play in any key.

The **numeric formula** for a major scale is **1–2–3–4–5–6–7**. The **root** (also called the **tonic**) is scale degree 1.

Major Scale Shape 1

Here's our first shape, which we'll play with its root on string 3 using our second finger. In second position, this is a C major scale:

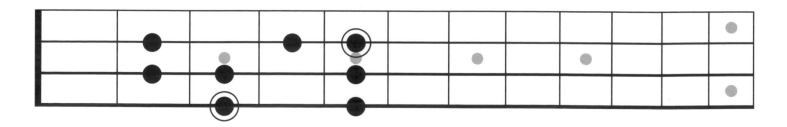

By the way, in each of these scale diagrams, the roots will be circled.

Now, we can also move this shape down a string set so the root is on string 4. Staying in second position, this will be a G major scale:

Of course, we can also move this shape laterally to any position on the neck to play from a different root. If we slide the third-string-root version up to fourth position, for example, we have a D major scale, because we're starting on a D root (string 3, fret 5).

Major Scale Shape 1 Examples

This is an extremely common scale shape and is used often in creating bass lines. Let's look at a few examples. Our first is in the key of C. It's a simple line that moves from the I chord, C, to the IV chord, F, using the same arpeggio pattern.

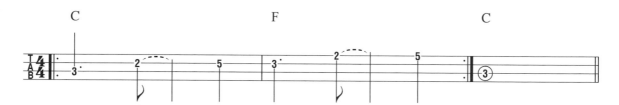

And here's another way to navigate a I–IV change. This one is in the key of A and is based on the scale shape with its root on string 4.

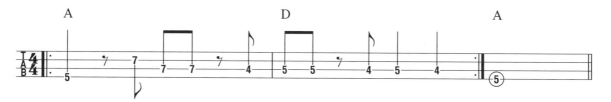

This next one demonstrates a common descending bass line in G. We're simply descending straight down the scale here. Take note of the chords that are implied; it's important to be aware of the chords you're playing beneath so that you'll know what notes will work best when you want to improvise a fill or two.

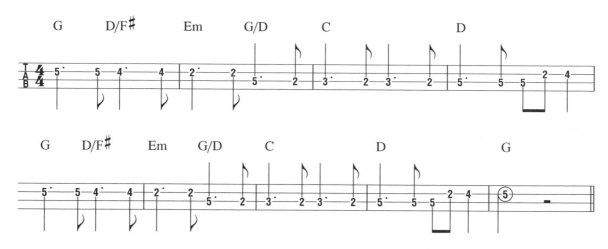

Ace session bassist Carol Kaye worked out of this shape in B major for the famous intro to "California Girls" by the Beach Boys.

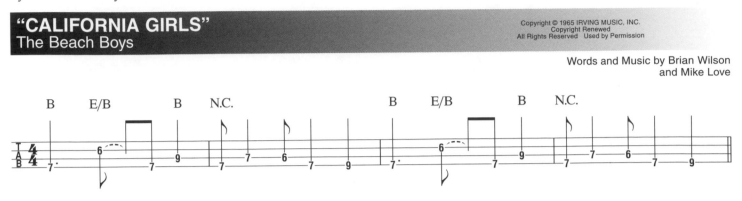

"CALIFORNIA GIRLS"
The Beach Boys

Words and Music by Brian Wilson
and Mike Love

In Eric Clapton's "Lay Down Sally," bassist Carl Radle camps out in this shape (in A major) for the entire chorus.

"LAY DOWN SALLY"
Eric Clapton

Words and Music by Eric Clapton,
Marcy Levy and George Terry

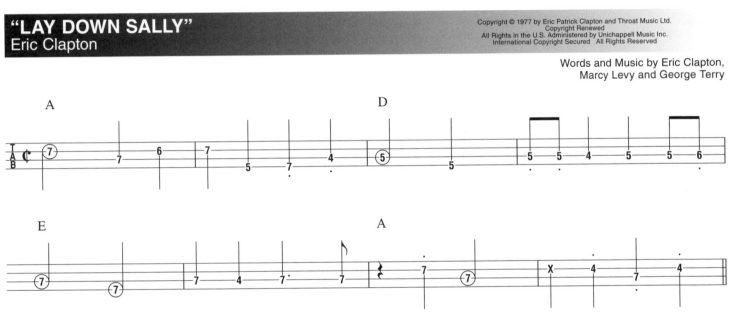

Major Scale Shape 2

Now let's check out our second major scale shape. This one uses our pinky on string 4 to play the root and uses all four strings.

We'll play this one is C as well, and we'll also add two commonly used scale notes below the root, since they are easily available in this position.

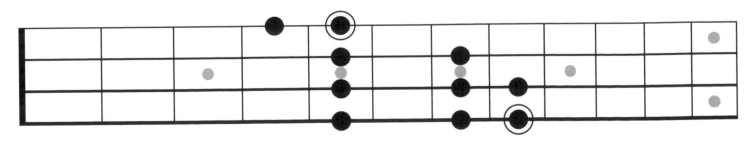

Again, you can move this shape anywhere up or down the neck to play in any key. Let's check out how it's used in some bass lines.

Major Scale Shape 2 Examples

We'll start with one in C that shows yet another way to connect the I chord to the IV chord. Can you see how the scale shape frames this line?

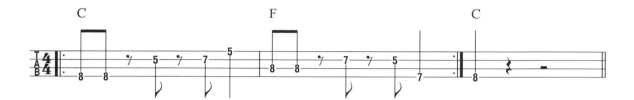

And here's kind of a funky groove in D that uses a few dead notes.

The Minor Scale

All right, now let's check out the depressed sibling of the major scale: the minor scale. The minor scale sounds dark, dramatic, and sometimes gothic.

Its numeric formula is 1–2–♭3–4–5–♭6–♭7.

Again we'll check out two different fingerings for it.

Minor Scale Shape 1

The first shape we'll look at has the first finger on the root and can be played off the fourth string or third string, since it covers only three strings. We'll play it in C minor here, which will put us in eighth position.

Just as with shape 1 of the major scale, we can move this shape up a string set, which, in this case, would create an F minor scale. When we play it on this string set, notice that we can add three notes below the root on string 4.

Minor Scale Shape 1 Examples

So let's check out this scale shape in action with a few bass lines. This one's easy to visualize because of its box-like shape.

 In this first example, we'll navigate a minor i–iv progression in C minor, which would be Cm to Fm. Notice how we exploit the same pattern on strings 4 and 3.

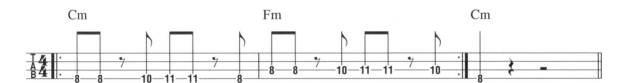

 Here's one in E minor with the root on string 3, which puts us in seventh position. We make use of some notes below the root, on string 4, for the final part of the line.

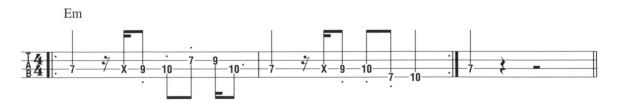

Steve Bossen lays it down for Heart in the classic "Barracuda," working out of this shape in E minor, with its root on string 4. He's playing in open position here, so the shape is harder to recognize, but if you imagine another fretted note in place of the open string, you can see it's the same shape.

"BARRACUDA"
Heart

Words and Music by Nancy Wilson, Ann Wilson,
Michael Derosier and Roger Fisher

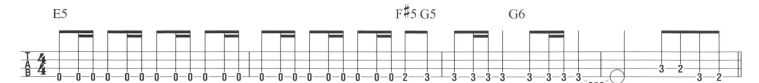

During the chorus of "Dream On," Aerosmith bassist Tom Hamilton works out of this shape in F# minor. Sometimes sustained root notes are all that's needed!

"DREAM ON"
Aerosmith

Words and Music by
Steven Tyler

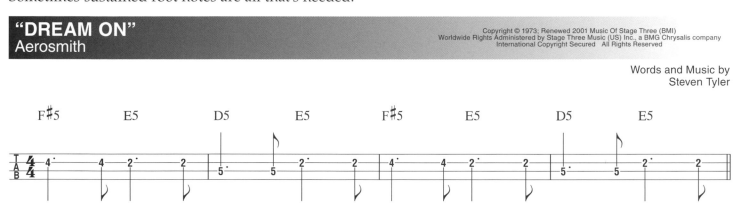

Minor Scale Shape 2

Similar to our major scale shape 2, our second minor scale shape also puts our fourth finger on the root, located on string 4. Here it is in C minor, with one note added below the low root.

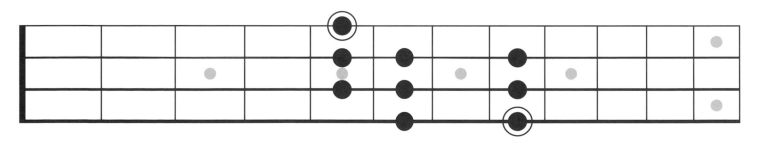

We can also move this shape up a string set so that the root is on string 3. We don't have access to as many notes above it, but we do have the added bonus of notes below it. The 5th below is especially nice and commonly used. If we remain in fifth position, this will give us an F minor scale.

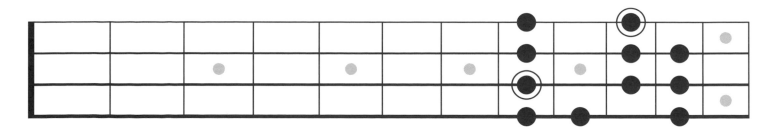

9

Minor Scale Shape 2 Examples

Now let's put this scale form into action with some bass lines. This next one is in D minor and stays on the bottom two strings throughout. The syncopation really propels this one.

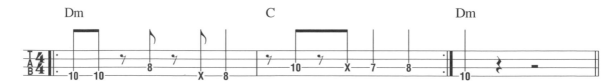

Here's a funky one in A minor that uses every note in the scale shape.

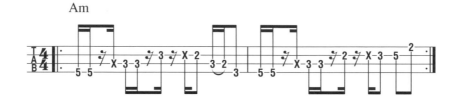

The verse of Marvin Gaye's "What's Going On" vamps between Emaj7 and C#m7. Over the C#m7, James Jamerson works his magic out of this shape with the root on string 3. Check out the characteristic sixteenth-note syncopated rhythms and the chromatic passing tone on string 3, fret 3.

"WHAT'S GOING ON"
Marvin Gaye

Words and Music by Renaldo Benson,
Alfred Cleveland and Marvin Gaye

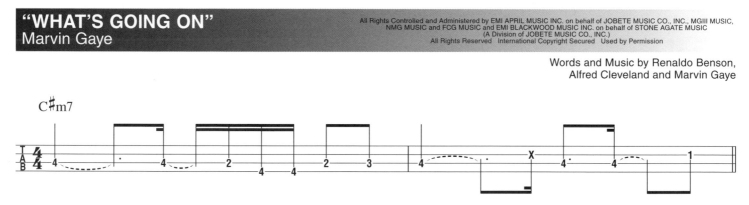

Check out how Gene Simmons works within this shape, also in C# minor, to pull off some speedy triplet-laced fills in Kiss's "Detroit Rock City."

"DETROIT ROCK CITY"
Kiss

Words and Music by Paul Stanley
and Bob Ezrin

Tune down 1/2 step:
(low to high) E♭–A♭–D♭–G♭

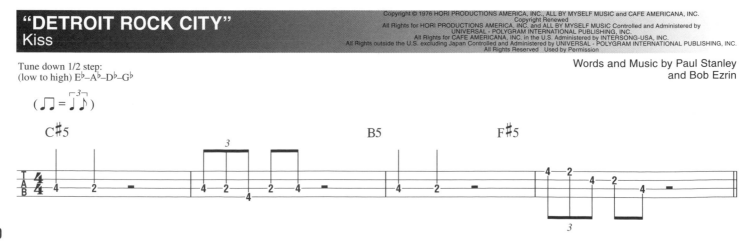

Scale Review

Let's finish up with a review of all the scale shapes we learned:

Major Scale Shape 1

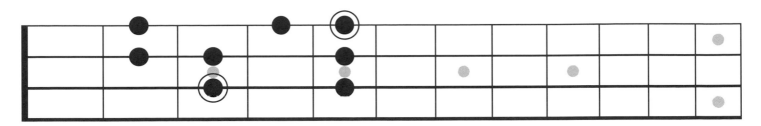

Major Scale Shape 2

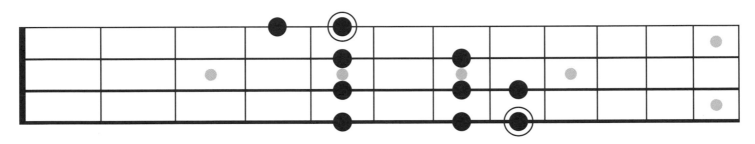

Minor Scale Shape 1

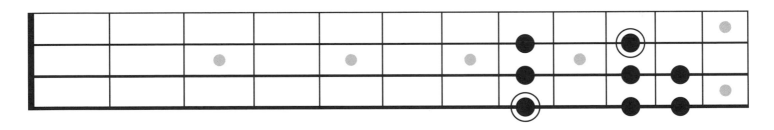

Minor Scale Shape 2

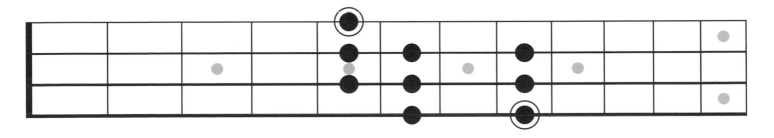

That does it for this lesson. Remember that all of these scale shapes can be moved up and down the neck, and many can be transferred to another string set as well.

PENTATONIC SCALE SHAPES

Take almost any famous bass line, and you can rest assured that it was created using the notes of a scale. We already checked out major and minor scales. Let's now explore pentatonic scales, which have been a favorite in many genres. In this lesson, we'll take a look at two of the most common—the major and minor pentatonic scales—and learn how to play them on bass. We'll also learn some great bass lines in the process.

What Is a Pentatonic Scale?

A scale is a collection of notes that we use to form melodies, chords, or bass lines. Though most scales have seven notes, **pentatonic** scales, as the name "penta" implies, have five.

The Major Pentatonic Scale

Let's start with the major pentatonic scale. We'll learn two different shapes, each of which can be moved any-where on the neck to play in any key.

The **numeric formula** for a major pentatonic scale is **1–2–3–5–6**.

Major Pentatonic Scale Shape 1

Here's our first shape, which we'll play with its root on string 3 using our second finger. In second position, this is a C major pentatonic scale.

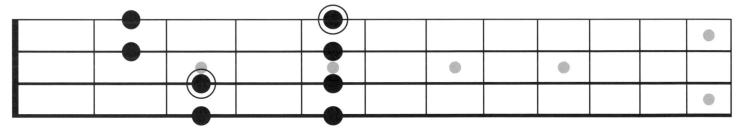

Notice that we've added two notes, the 5th and 6th, on string 4 below the root. Since no open strings are involved, this is a **moveable shape**. We can move it down a string set so the root is on string 4. Staying in second position, this will be a G major pentatonic scale. In this shape, above the high root, we've added the 2nd and 3rd notes of the scale on string 1.

Of course, we can also move this shape laterally to any position on the neck to play from a different root. If we slide the third-string-root version up to fourth position, for example, we have a D major pentatonic scale.

Major Pentatonic Scale Shape 1 Examples

This is a great shape and is used often in Motown styles. Let's look at a few examples. Our first is in the key of C and demonstrates a classic Motown-style major pentatonic line.

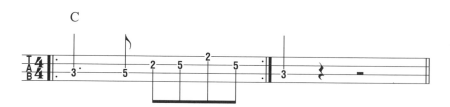

Here's another idea in the key of D. Here, we're moving the same scale form, with its root on string 4, to play the same line over the I, V, and IV chords: D, A, and G.

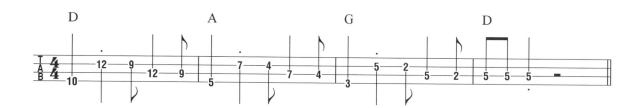

Many bass lines have been built using the 5th, 6th, and root of the scale, as demonstrated in this next example. Here, we're just moving the third-string root form from D up to G and back.

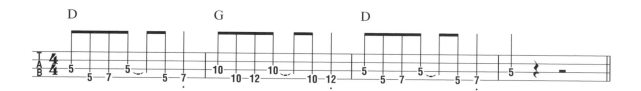

In Elvis's "All Shook Up," Bill Black transposes this shape for each of the chords—D, E, and A—and lets his fingers do the walking.

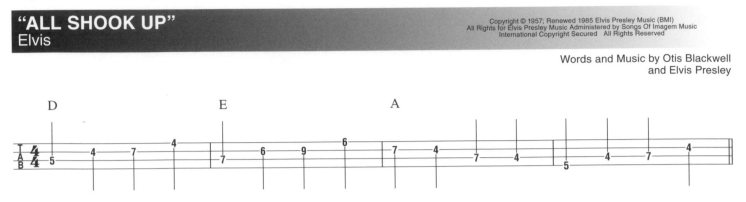

"ALL SHOOK UP"
Elvis

Words and Music by Otis Blackwell
and Elvis Presley

James Jamerson gives a masterful lesson on how you can smoothly combine two different shapes in Smokey Robinson's "I Second That Emotion." The entire verse takes place over a D chord, but check out the two-measure pattern that Jamerson plays, which, as is often the case, becomes a hook in its own right. For the first measure, he's working right out of shape 1.

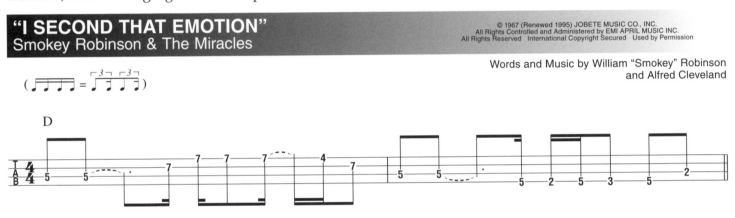

"I SECOND THAT EMOTION"
Smokey Robinson & The Miracles

Words and Music by William "Smokey" Robinson
and Alfred Cleveland

Major Pentatonic Scale Shape 2

Now let's check out our second major pentatonic shape. This employs our pinky on string 4 to play the root and uses all four strings.

We'll play this one in C as well, adding a note on top above the high root and one on the bottom below the low root.

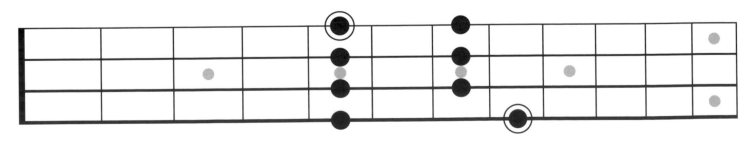

Again, you can move this shape anywhere up or down the neck to play in any key. Let's check out how it's used in some bass lines.

Major Pentatonic Scale Shape 2 Examples

We'll start with one in C that makes a nice use of the low 6th tone—A in this case.

Here's a funky groove in E that uses a few dead notes and again stresses the low 6th tone.

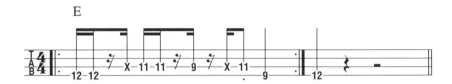

Jamerson strikes again in the Marvin Gaye/Tammi Terrell duet "Ain't Nothing Like the Real Thing." Check out how he grooves like only he can in E♭, working right out of shape 2. The final A note leads smoothly down to the IV chord, A♭, which follows (not shown).

"AIN'T NOTHING LIKE THE REAL THING"
Marvin Gaye & Tammi Terrell

Words and Music by Nickolas Ashford
and Valerie Simpson

The Minor Pentatonic Scale

All right, now let's look at the dark side: the minor pentatonic scale. This scale is commonly used in blues rock, especially.

Its **numeric formula** is 1–♭3–4–5–♭7.

Again, we'll check out two different fingerings for it.

Minor Pentatonic Scale Shape 1

The first shape we'll look at has the first finger on the root and is played off string 4. It contains two extra notes above the top root that are used fairly often. We'll play it in C minor here, which will put us in eighth position.

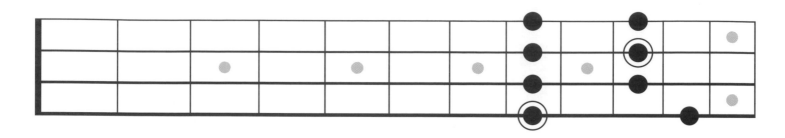

You may have noticed that this looks just like our major pentatonic shape 2. And that's right; it's the same shape. The difference is that here we're treating the C note as the root of the scale.

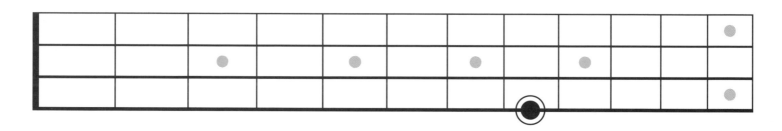

Whereas in the major pentatonic, this E♭ note would be treated as the root.

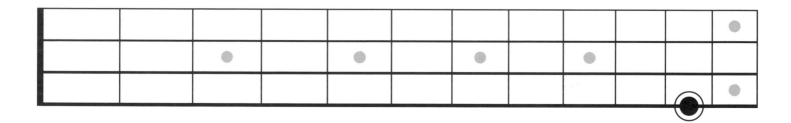

So the only difference really lies in how we use the pattern. Let's check out this minor pentatonic scale shape in action with a few bass lines.

Minor Pentatonic Scale Shape 1 Examples

Here's a shuffle example in A minor played in fifth position. The beginning is repeated, but the ending is different.

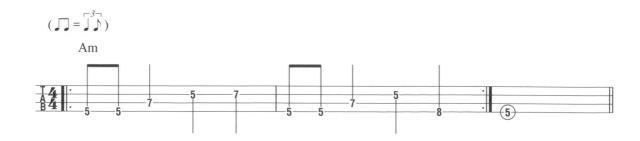

16

This one's in B minor and makes use of the additional top two notes in a question-and-answer format.

In the immortal rock classic "Smoke on the Water," Deep Purple bassist Roger Glover riffs out of shape 1 in G minor pentatonic, only briefing dropping down to first position to cover the F5 chord.

"SMOKE ON THE WATER"
Deep Purple

Words and Music by Ritchie Blackmore, Ian Gillan, Roger Glover, Jon Lord and Ian Paice

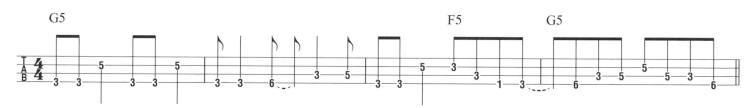

Minor Pentatonic Scale Shape 2

Similar to our major pentatonic scale shape 2, our second minor pentatonic shape also puts our fourth finger on the root of string 4. Here it is in C minor, with one note added below the low root and one added on top, above the high root.

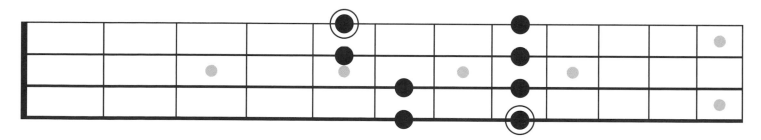

We can move this shape up a string set as well, so that the root lies on string 3. We don't have a full octave on top, but we get access to some great notes on bottom. Here it is in fifth position as an F minor pentatonic.

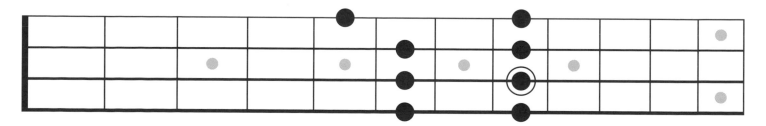

Now let's put this scale form into action with some bass lines.

17

Minor Pentatonic Scale Shape 2 Examples

Here's a rolling bass line in D minor that uses only the bottom two strings of the shape.

Here's a hooky line in E minor that contrasts the low register of the scale with the higher in another question-and-answer phrase.

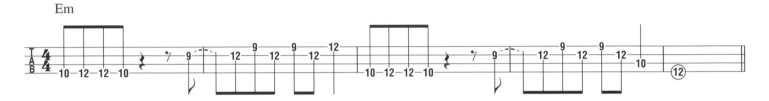

Alec John Such fuel's the arena rock of Bon Jovi's "You Give Love a Bad Name" with a C# minor pentatonic riff of undulating eighth notes.

Words and Music by Jon Bon Jovi,
Desmond Child and Richie Sambora

Tune down 1/2 step:
(low to high) E♭–A♭–D♭–G♭

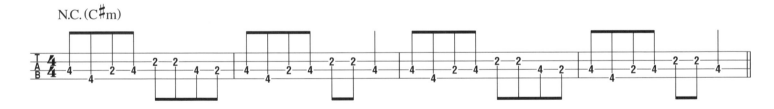

The Dire Straits classic "Sultans of Swing" begins on a groove in Dm, and bassist John Illsley exhibits tasteful restraint working from shape 2 of the D minor pentatonic scale.

"SULTANS OF SWING"
Dire Straits

Words and Music by
Mark Knopfler

Scale Review

Let's finish up with a review of all the scale shapes we learned:

Major Pentatonic Scale Shape 1

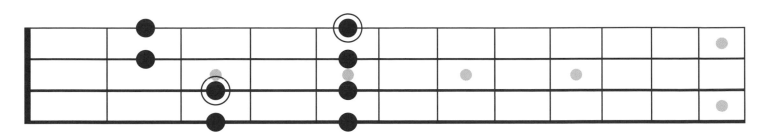

Major Pentatonic Scale Shape 2

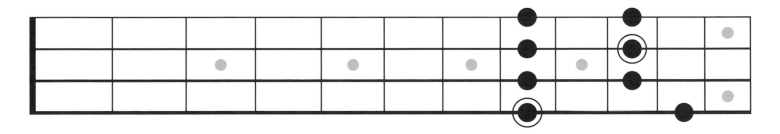

Minor Pentatonic Scale Shape 1

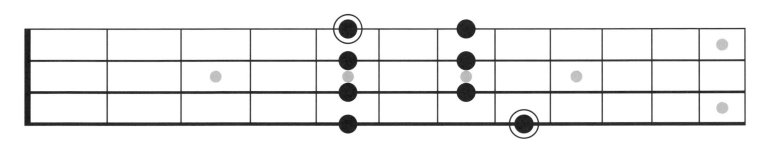

Minor Pentatonic Scale Shape 2

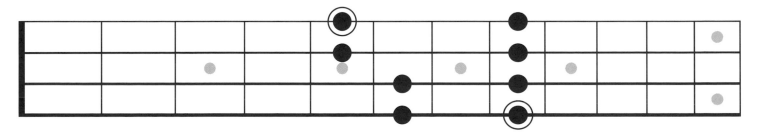

That's it for this lesson. Be sure to practice these scale shapes in other keys by moving them up and down to different places on the neck.

THE SEVEN MODES

If you've got the major and minor scales down and you're wanting to expand your tonal palette a bit, it's time to check out the **modes**. In this lesson, we'll examine the seven modes and learn how they can be used to create some catchy bass lines.

What Are the Modes?

Though modes are widely misunderstood, they don't need to be. You just need to understand some basic theory. There are seven diatonic modes:

Ionian

Dorian

Phrygian

Lydian

Mixolydian

Aeolian

Locrian

There are two ways you can view the modes. We'll look at each in this lesson.

Parent Major Scale Approach

The first is to relate them to a parent major scale. To demonstrate, let's a play a C major scale: C–D–E–F–G–A–B.

By doing that, you've actually just played your first mode. The Ionian mode is simply another name for the major scale. So:

C Major Scale = C Ionian Mode

Also, the Aeolian mode is the same as the relative minor scale. So, C Ionian is the C major scale, and A Aeolian is the A minor scale. Another way to say this is that we're playing the notes of a C major scale but treating A (the sixth note) as the root.

A Aeolian = A Minor Scale

Now, if we play the same C major scale notes, but treat the second note, D, as the root, we're playing a different mode: D Dorian.

We can continue like this through the whole C major scale. Treating the note, E, as the root, we get the E Phrygian mode, and so on.

So the seven modes of C major are:

C Ionian

D Dorian

E Phrygian

F Lydian

G Mixolydian

A Aeolian

B Locrian

Without some kind of context, however, all of these modes will pretty much sound like the C major scale. This is a somewhat academic way of viewing the modes, because the difference between them is mostly on paper— i.e., you can't really hear it.

Separate Scale Approach

The other approach involves viewing *each mode as a separate scale*, each with its own numeric formula.

Ionian Mode

The numeric formula for the major scale, or Ionian mode, is the standard by which we measure all others. The formula is: 1–2–3–4–5–6–7.

In C, this would be: C–D–E–F–G–A–B.

Since this scale contains a major 3rd, it's called a major mode. By altering this formula, we can create other scales or modes.

The Ionian mode is everywhere in popular music. Here's an example of Brian Wilson's line in the Beach Boys classic, "Surfin' U.S.A." Note that, though it starts on B♭, this is actually the V chord, and the song is in the key of E♭, which is confirmed immediately in measure 3.

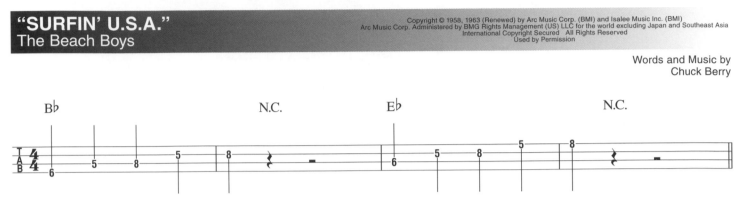

Words and Music by
Chuck Berry

Aeolian Mode

The Aeolian mode is simply another name for the minor scale. From a major scale, we need to lower the 3rd, 6th, and 7th degrees. Therefore, its numeric formula is 1–2–♭3–4–5–♭6–♭7.

In C, this would be: C–D–E♭–F–G–A♭–B♭.

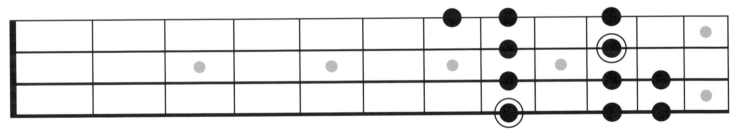

With a ♭3rd degree, this is a minor mode.

Dorian Mode

If we flat or lower the 3rd and 7th degrees of the Ionian Mode (major scale) by a half step, we'll end up with a C Dorian mode.

So the numeric formula for Dorian is 1–2–♭3–4–5–6–♭7. In C, that's C–D–E♭–F–G–A–B♭.

Here's a common fingering for C Dorian around eighth position:

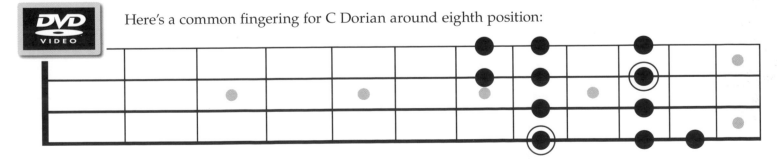

Since Dorian contains a minor 3rd (E♭ in this case), it's a minor mode.

Dorian Examples

Let's check out a few bass lines built from the C Dorian mode.

Notice how the major 6th tone, A, adds a brightness to the minor harmony.

 Here's another example that's a bit funkier.

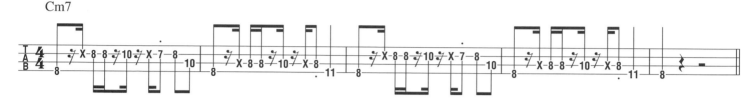

Dave Hope works out of the A Dorian mode for the famous ensemble riff in the Kansas hit "Carry On Wayward Son." He's combining two adjacent scale forms here, with the one we've looked at appearing in measure 2. The F♯ note at the very end of the phrase is the tell-tale sign that we're in A Dorian here.

"CARRY ON WAYWARD SON"
Kansas

Words and Music by
Kerry Livgren

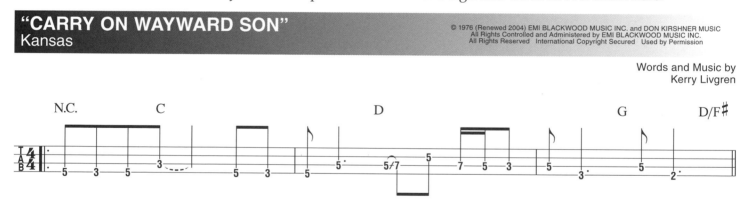

Mixolydian Mode

If we take a C Ionian mode and flat the 7th degree, we get C Mixolydian. Therefore, the numeric formula for Mixolydian is 1–2–3–4–5–6–♭7. In C, that's C–D–E–F–G–A–B♭.

And here's a fingering for C Mixolydian.

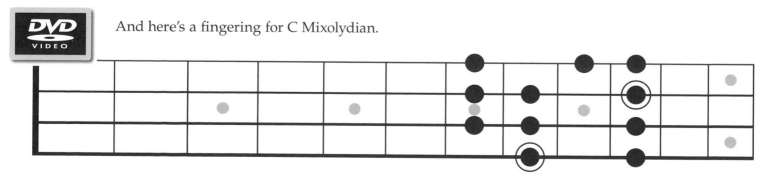

This one contains a major 3rd, E, so it's another major mode; more specifically, it's a dominant mode because it also contains the ♭7th.

Mixolydian Examples

Let's check out some C Mixolydian bass lines. Here's a nice one that grooves well.

Here's another that uses a question-and-answer format. Only the last two notes are reversed each time.

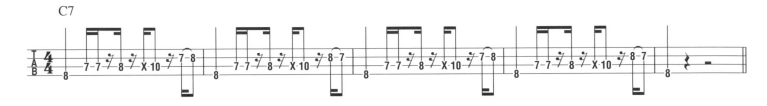

Aerosmith bassist Tom Hamilton made use of the A Mixolydian mode to craft one of the most famous bass intros in all of rock for "Sweet Emotion." Note that he's using a scale pattern here with its root on string 3 instead of string 4. To get this shape, you basically just shift the form over one string set.

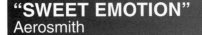

"SWEET EMOTION"
Aerosmith

Words and Music by Steven Tyler
and Tom Hamilton

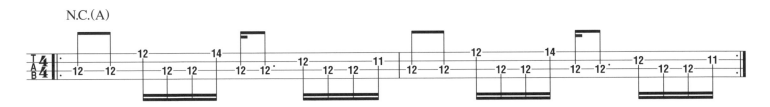

Lydian Mode

If we take the C Ionian mode and raise the 4th by a half step, we get the C Lydian mode. So the numeric formula for Lydian is 1–2–3–#4–5–6–7. In C, that's C–D–E–F#–G–A–B.

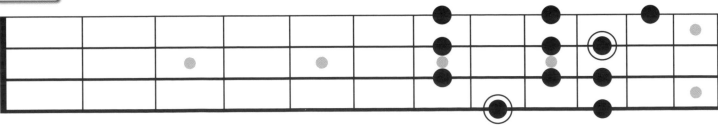

This is a very bright-sounding mode that's not terribly common in pop music, but it does crop up occasionally.

Lydian Example

Let's check out a C Lydian bass line. The #4th really grabs your ear.

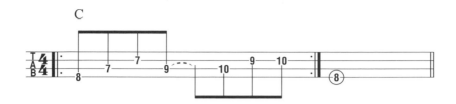

We covered Dorian, Mixolydian, and Lydian first because they're the most commonly used—aside from Ionian and Aeolian, of course, which you already know.

Phrygian Mode

You also occasionally see the Phrygian mode. Its numeric formula is 1–♭2–♭3–4–5–♭6–♭7. In C, that's C–D♭–E♭–F–G–A♭–B♭.

Here's C Phrygian:

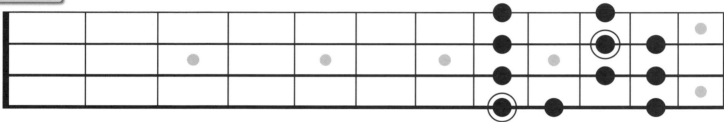

Phrygian Example

This is another minor mode, but the ♭2nd makes it pretty sinister-sounding, so it tends to see a lot of action in metal. You'll hear things like this sometimes.

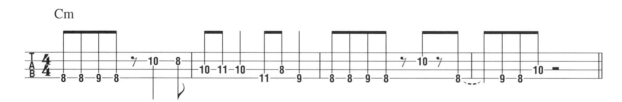

Alice in Chains bassist Mike Starr worked from the F♯ Phrygian mode for the verse of "Would?" Notice that he's making use of the low ♭7th note (E, in this case) for an extra bit of grunge muscle.

"WOULD?"
Alice in Chains

Written by Jerry Cantrell

Tune down 1/2 step:
(low to high) E♭–A♭–D♭–G♭

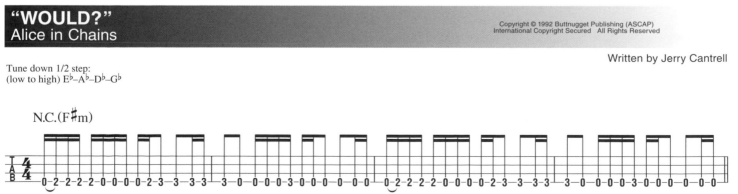

Locrian Mode

The final mode is Locrian. Since it contains a ♭3rd and a ♭5th, it's technically a diminished mode—or half-diminished, more specifically. Its numeric formula is 1–♭2–♭3–4–♭5–♭6–♭7. In C, that's C–D♭–E♭–F–G♭–A♭–B♭.

 It's rarely used outside of some jazz or more exotic metal. To be thorough, though, here's a fingering for C Locrian:

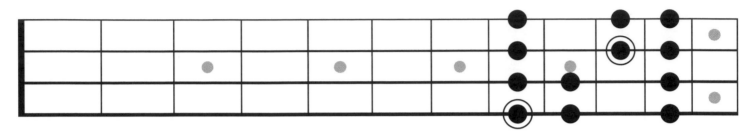

That's gonna do it for this lesson. Remember that these modes, just like any other scale, can be played all over the neck, so I encourage you to learn them that way. I hope you've enjoyed this modal journey; have fun coming up with your own ideas!

MIXOLYDIAN BASS GROOVES

Even if you don't think you know what the Mixolydian mode is, you've no doubt heard it in countless bass lines. From Motown to blues—from funk to rock—it's everywhere. In this lesson, we're going to learn the appeal of the Mixolydian bass groove.

Mixolydian Construction

We touched on the Mixolydian mode in the last lesson on the seven modes. Let's review quickly just to make sure you've got it straight. If you know your major scale, then you almost know the Mixolydian mode. In order to create a Mixolydian mode, we just need to flat, or lower by half step, the 7th degree of a major scale.

So, whereas a C major scale is spelled C–D–E–F–G–A–B, C Mixolydian is spelled C–D–E–F–G–A–B♭.

We can say, then, that the numeric formula for a Mixolydian mode is 1–2–3–4–5–6–♭7.

Mixolydian Scale Shape 1

Let's check out a common fingering for the C Mixolydian mode in seventh position. Our second finger handles the low root note on string 4.

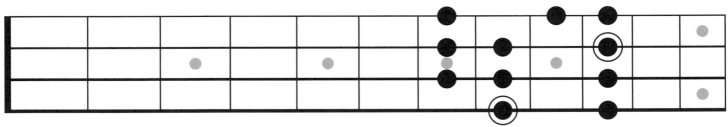

Since the scale forms presented in this lesson contain no open strings, they're moveable. So we can slide the same form up two frets, for instance, and we get D Mixolydian.

Let's check out our first groove using this scale form. This one is in C and sounds great beneath either a C or C7 chord.

Groove 1

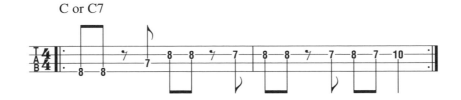

And here's one in A that's right at home in a bluesy shuffle.

Groove 2

In the Beatles classic "Paperback Writer," Paul McCartney riffs out of this shape in G Mixolydian. Note that he efficiently exploits the open A string during the ascending line of measure 2, though you could play the A note on string 4, fret 5 as well.

"PAPERBACK WRITER"
The Beatles

Words and Music by John Lennon
and Paul McCartney

Mixolydian Scale Shape 2

Here's another common Mixolydian fingering. This one uses our fourth finger on the low fourth-string root.

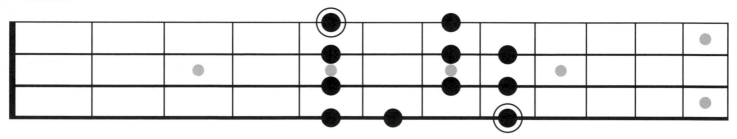

Now let's check out a funky groove in C using that form. This one uses a few dead notes and plenty of syncopation.

Groove 3

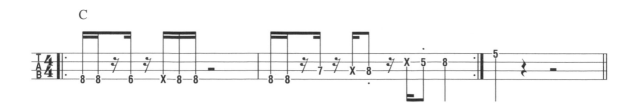

And here's one in E that's a bit more angular and slightly up-tempo.

Groove 4

Mixolydian Scale Shape 3

Of course, you can play these scale forms with their low roots based off string 3 as well. This allows us to add some additional notes below the root.

Here's C Mixolydian with our second finger on the low third-string root.

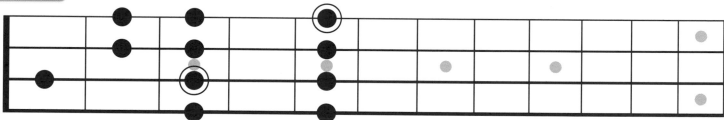

McCartney makes use of this shape for the immortal riff in "Day Tripper." A few things are of note here. First of all, notice how he approaches the major 3rd (G♯) from a half step below (G) on string 2, fret 5. Use your first finger for both of these notes. Secondly, he briefly shifts up for the high F♯ note in measure 2 before settling back into position to wrap up the two-measure phrase.

"DAY TRIPPER"
The Beatles

Words and Music by John Lennon
and Paul McCartney

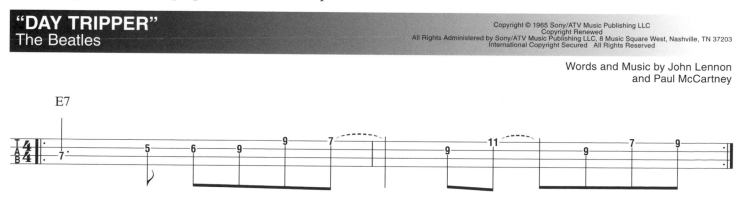

Mixolydian Scale Shape 4

And here's how Mixolydian looks with our fourth finger on the third-string root. We'll play this shape in D in order to avoid open strings for now. This one's nice because you have the low 3rd available on string 4, which can be used to great effect.

Here's a shuffling groove in C using scale form 3.

Groove 5

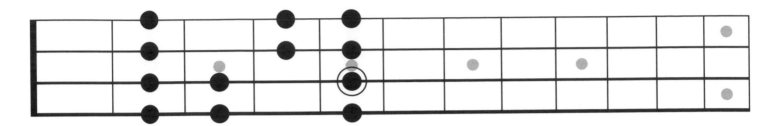

In this funky line in the key of F, we exploit the low 3rd available in form 4.

Groove 6

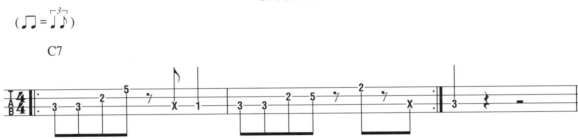

In Stevie Ray Vaughan's "Crossfire," bassist Tommy Shannon works out of this form to create the main hook of the song. Notice how he cleverly combines the open E string with shape 4 in fourth position.

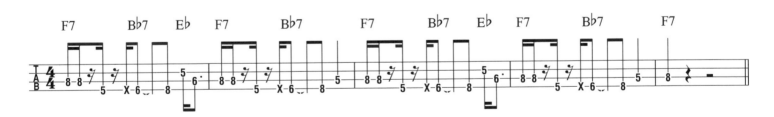

"CROSSFIRE"
Stevie Ray Vaughan and Double Trouble

Words and Music by Bill Carter, Ruth Ellsworth,
Reese Wynans, Tommy Shannon
and Chris Layton

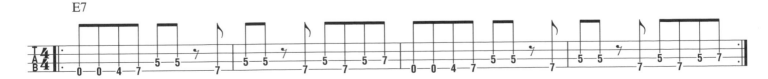

No one knows a Mixolydian groove better than Bootsy Collins, as he aptly demonstrates on the James Brown funk fest "Get Up (I Feel Like Being) A Sex Machine." He's working out of shape 4 of E♭ Mixolydian here, and the groove is thumpin'! Slow it down at first to really work out those syncopated sixteenth notes!

"GET UP (I FEEL LIKE BEING) A SEX MACHINE"
James Brown

Words and Music by James Brown,
Bobby Byrd and Ronald Lenhoff

I hope you've begun to get a handle on the Mixolydian mode and how useful it can be in generating bass grooves for many different styles. After you've gotten these grooves down, try varying a few notes here and there to come up with your own. Good luck!

BASS BUILDERS

A series of technique book/CD packages created for the purposeful building and development of your chops. Each volume is written by an expert in that particular technique. And with the inclusion of audio, the added dimension of hearing exactly how to play particular grooves and techniques make these truly like private lessons.

BASS AEROBICS
by Jon Liebman
00696437 Book/CD Pack..........$19.99

BASS FITNESS – AN EXERCISING HANDBOOK
by Josquin des Prés
00660177..........$10.99

BASS FOR BEGINNERS
by Glenn Letsch
00695099 Book/CD Pack..........$19.95

BASS GROOVES
by Jon Liebman
00696028 Book/CD Pack..........$19.99

BASS IMPROVISATION
by Ed Friedland
00695164 Book/CD Pack..........$17.95

BLUES BASS
by Jon Liebman
00695235 Book/CD Pack..........$19.95

BUILDING ROCK BASS LINES
by Ed Friedland
00695692 Book/CD Pack..........$17.95

BUILDING WALKING BASS LINES
by Ed Friedland
00695008 Book/CD Pack..........$19.99

RON CARTER – BUILDING JAZZ BASS LINES
00841240 Book/CD Pack..........$19.95

DICTIONARY OF BASS GROOVES
by Sean Malone
00695266 Book/CD Pack..........$14.95

EXPANDING WALKING BASS LINES
by Ed Friedland
00695026 Book/CD Pack..........$19.95

FINGERBOARD HARMONY FOR BASS
by Gary Willis
00695043 Book/CD Pack..........$17.95

FUNK BASS
by Jon Liebman
00699348 Book/CD Pack..........$19.99

FUNK/FUSION BASS
by Jon Liebman
00696553 Book/CD Pack..........$19.95

HIP-HOP BASS
by Josquin des Prés
00695589 Book/CD Pack..........$14.95

JAZZ BASS
by Ed Friedland
00695084 Book/CD Pack..........$17.95

JERRY JEMMOTT – BLUES AND RHYTHM & BLUES BASS TECHNIQUE
00695176 Book/CD Pack..........$17.95

JUMP 'N' BLUES BASS
by Keith Rosier
00695292 Book/CD Pack..........$16.95

THE LOST ART OF COUNTRY BASS
by Keith Rosier
00695107 Book/CD Pack..........$19.95

PENTATONIC SCALES FOR BASS
by Ed Friedland
00696224 Book/CD Pack..........$19.99

REGGAE BASS
by Ed Friedland
00695163 Book/CD Pack..........$16.95

ROCK BASS
by Jon Liebman
00695083 Book/CD Pack..........$17.95

'70S FUNK & DISCO BASS
by Josquin des Prés
00695614 Book/CD Pack..........$15.99

SIMPLIFIED SIGHT-READING FOR BASS
by Josquin des Prés
00695085 Book/CD Pack..........$17.95

6-STRING BASSICS
by David Gross
00695221 Book/CD Pack..........$12.95

SLAP BASS ESSENTIALS
by Josquin dés Pres and Bunny Brunel
00696563 Book/CD Pack..........$19.95

WORLD BEAT GROOVES FOR BASS
by Tony Cimorosi
00695335 Book/CD Pack..........$14.95

HAL•LEONARD® CORPORATION

7777 W. BLUEMOUND RD. P.O. BOX 13819 MILWAUKEE, WI 53213

Visit Hal Leonard Online at www.halleonard.com

Prices, contents and availability subject to change without notice; All prices are listed in U.S. funds

1112